The Catholic
DIVORCE
SURVIVAL
Guide

Helping You Find
Peace, Power, and Passion
After Your Divorce

Personal Survival Guide

SAINT
BENEDICT
PRESS

ISBN: 978-1-935302-55-1

Book design by A.R.T. Services, Christopher J. Pelicano.

Printed and bound in the United States of America.

SAINT
BENEDICT
PRESS

Saint Benedict Press, LLC
Charlotte, North Carolina

2012

Welcome
to the *Catholic's DIVORCE SURVIVAL Guide*

This Survival Guide is a short summary of our series to help you remember the key points of every show.

Maybe you're going through divorce now—or perhaps it has been some time, even years ago now, and you're still struggling with certain issues. No matter where you are, we can help.

We can't cover every issue in this series, but we'll try to cover the most important, and for additional resources you can always visit our Web site:

www.FaithLifeline.com

You'll listen and learn from Catholic men and women like you who share their stories of finding help and healing. We also feature Catholic experts in counseling, spiritual direction, and Church teachings to help you navigate your way out of the desert of divorce.

About Peace, Power, and Passion
... after all, most people just want PEACE

And almost everyone wants to hang on to a sense of POWER ... power to maintain your dignity and to get what is due you after divorce, power to win, to stay "in control," even if only for the sake of the kids. But stop and think: this thirst for power may be part of what leads to divorce in the first place.

And then there's PASSION. We'd be happy again if we could only find someone to love us again, to hold us and kiss us and fill the empty place in our heart.

But it is Christ who is Perfect PEACE.

It is Jesus who shows us that true POWER is in forgiveness, humility, longsuffering, and sacrifice.

It is Jesus Christ who is faithful, never-ending Love. He alone can show us PASSION in a Love that truly satisfies.

Our series is set apart into these three areas, so if you've lost peace, power, or passion through your divorce, we can help.

We know what you want.
... and we'll help you find it

Your Catholic's DIVORCE SURVIVAL guides:

Rose Sweet: Catholic speaker and author of Healing the Divorced Heart and Dear God Send Me a Soul Mate
www.RoseSweet.com

Christopher West: Theologian, husband, father, and author of The Good News about Sex and Marriage
www.ChristopherWest.com

Dr. Ray Guarendi: Catholic author, psychologist, father of ten, and host of radio talk show "The Doctor Is In"
www.DrRay.com

Father Donald Calloway: Catholic priest and author, himself a child of divorce
www.FatherCalloway.com

Father Steve Porter: Catholic priest and seasoned Spiritual Director
www.FrSteve.tv

Father Mitch Pacwa: Catholic priest, author, and favorite host on EWTN
www.IgnatiusProductions.com

The Church Is Here to Help

Some people have been chastised, neglected, or deeply wounded by someone in the Catholic Church. As a result, they harbor mistrust; some have even left the Church.

But if you are one of those people, please don't leave Peter because of Judas.

Despite what you may have experienced, the Catholic Church is not here to condemn, but to console, and to help you and your family find peace, power, and renewed passion for life.

Let us help you through this tough time and show you the true love that is still in Christ's Church.

PART 1

Finding Perfect Peace

Session 1: Getting Your Bearings
Session 2: Finding Strength and Help
Session 3: Getting through Your Anger
Session 4: Finding Perfect Peace

I once witnessed my brother, a respected surgeon, perform surgery on a young boy who had torn open his leg just below the knee in a playground accident. He'd been to the ER a few days before and had been stitched up and sent home, but after a few days his mother noticed a high fever and inflammation in the leg. Now the boy was back on the table, and when my brother reopened the wound, he saw that it had not been thoroughly cleaned out the first time: there was still gravel in the boy's leg, and now even more healthy tissue had been damaged. So my brother had to cut deeper into the flesh, flush out the wound again, remove the dead tissue, and put in additional stitches.

The lesson? When we rush to clean up the emotional wounds left by divorce and don't take the time or work required to uncover and address all the problems, they will just fester until we have a relapse, that will leave much more damage than before.

Let us help you stabilize, doing it right the first time!

Shock and Denial Are Normal

Shock and denial are built-in safety mechanisms that keep us from going insane! They can provide a transition period after a trauma so that the mind and body can collect themselves and begin to face, slowly and carefully, the reality of what is happening.

The trouble starts when we are so afraid to face reality that we stay stuck in this phase of normal grief and recovery.

Personal Reflections:

Uncover all problems to prevent reoccurance

- Self blame
- anger
- Goal oriented

Worry and Fear May Overwhelm You

Divorce is a terrible collection of losses; at some point you may feel completely drained and overwhelmed, unable even to move. Remember that these are feelings (not always consistent with reality), and that feelings come and go, changing from day to day.

This is a time to try to stick close to what you know to be true, not to the feelings you have today. Don't repress your emotions, but also don't let them take charge of your life.

Personal Reflections:

Allow reason and faith to guide our emotions.

St. Ignatious "we are not responsibly for our emotions." We need to go higher

_____

_____

_____

_____

_____

_____

_____

_____

_____

_____

_____

_____

_____

_____

_____

_____

_____

_____

_____

_____

Your Healing Must Come First

A common tendency for divorced people is to busy themselves with their daily routine, worrying about the kids, keeping on as if nothing happened. But divorce is like a terrible car crash where a whole family is injured. The wounds of divorce may not be visible, but the internal bleeding of the emotions must be addressed.

You must help the kids, but you won't be able to give them what they need until you put on an emotional tourniquet and stop your own emotional bleeding. If you don't, a major relapse is sure to follow after which everyone might be even worse off.

Personal Reflections:

Don't rush to the next
relationship. Take time to
know self.

Healing Always Takes Time

Rushing through your recovery and latching onto something . . . or someone . . . that will make you feel better may be the worst thing you can do in the long run.

Just like a physical recovery, uncovering years of damaged emotions (that may have been there even before you married!) and getting healthy bearings takes time.

Don't rush.

Personal Reflections:

Do not expect some resurgence.

_____

_____

_____

_____

_____

_____

Only God Can Bring Full Healing

Divorce can force you to stop and take a look at what is really important in life. I never knew how many things I'd made into "false idols": my marriage, being a mom, having a nice home, planning for the future. I always asked God to bless my needs and wants, but I never really put Him first.

Through my divorce I discovered two things: (1) I can't heal myself, all by myself, on my own terms, and (2) what my heart had always longed for was not people and things . . . but Him.

Only God can satisfy the deepest desires of your heart, and only He can bring full healing from your divorce.

Personal Reflections:

_____

_____

_____

_____

_____

_____

1. Don't Let Feelings Take Charge

After divorce, most of our energies go to our wounded emotions. But feelings aren't facts.

Learn to step over emotions; let them come and go, and learn instead to "go higher," to the intellect. Feelings change, but Truth never does.

Give big decisions time . . . and wait for God's direction.

2. Change Your Busy Schedule

Busyness can be good in that it keeps us from wallowing in self pity, but it can also distract us from hearing God's voice and numb us to the pain that is meant to teach us something important.

Drop all unnecessary activity for at least a few months.

Eat well and stay rested. Get a little exercise.

_____

_____

_____

3. Draw Closer to Our Lord

Start with simple prayer, whenever you can, like . . . "Help!"

He's real, and He's here—and He knows exactly what you need, and He desires to give it to you.

St. Teresa of Avila was a fiery and intelligent Carmelite nun who fell madly in love with Love Himself. She writes:

Let nothing trouble you. Let nothing frighten you. All things are passing. God never changes. Patience gains all things. Whoever has God wants for nothing. God alone is enough.

_____

_____

_____

_____

_____

_____

_____

_____

Don't Look Around for Love

Looking for love in a bar—or anywhere else, for that matter—is common, but really it's plain stupid.

As soon as we lose something precious, our instinct is to quickly grab hold of something of someone to keep us happy.

Most of us look frantically for peace, power, and passion, but we really haven't discovered what True Love really is!

Give yourself some time to learn. This is a time when God wants to show you how to obtain what you really need and want. Look to Him.

Personal Reflections:

_____

_____

_____

_____

_____

_____

SESSION 2 – SURVIVAL POINT 2
Don't Give in to Loneliness

Loneliness is a powerful emotion that can drive you to despair, but emotions come and go, changing with the wind.

The fear of being alone can drive us to look for love even in places that seem okay. After divorce, some people naturally run to the Church and find comfort there, but the same emotional neediness that drives us to the bars can have us looking around in the pews. We think a person who goes to church is safe, but that's not always the case. Be careful.

Personal Reflections:

_____

_____

_____

_____

_____

_____

_____

_____

_____

_____

_____

_____

_____

_____

_____

_____

_____

_____

_____

_____

_____

_____

_____

_____

_____

_____

_____

Look for Help from the Church

Imagine the Church as a hospital; you can get over-the-counter help for small issues in other places, but the fullest healing for the deepest wounds comes only from the Sacraments.

The Sacraments are personal and powerful encounters with Jesus Himself. They impart graces and power—and hope!

There's no substitute for baring your soul to a loving God in Confession, receiving the soothing balm of His mercy, and then receiving Him into your very self in the Eucharist.

Wow! That's deeply personal "communion."

Personal Reflections:

_____

_____

_____

_____

_____

_____

Make an Interim Plan

Scripture says that without a plan the people perish (Proverbs 29:18). God also tells us to write helpful and important things down (Habakkuk 2:2).

When we don't have a clear plan of what to do, we tend to panic, or to grab hold of bad things. In the aftermath of divorce, you may have to make a temporary plan for you and your family:

- Cut back on what's not necessary.
- Make time for reading helpful books, or for journaling.
- Find a good Catholic therapist or Spiritual Director (see, for example, www.CatholicTherapists.com).

Personal Reflections:

_____

_____

_____

_____

_____

_____

Look for Help from the Church

Jesus says, "Take my yoke upon you, for my yoke is easy and my burden is light." What does that really mean? Imagine a wooden yoke on the shoulders of two animals pulling side by side. God knows you will have to work through your divorce. There's no escaping it! He won't do it all for you, but He will do it with you.

And he promises to carry the bigger load!

Personal Reflections:

_____

_____

_____

_____

_____

_____

_____

1. Find Help in God's Word

There are no greater words of direction, advice, or consolation than those found in Scripture.

Go get your Bible off the shelf and start reading—even if only for a few minutes a day.

Start with the Psalms, where you'll read hearts' cries similar to your own.

Have pity on me, for I am fading away . . . my spirit is shaken to its very depths . . . rescue me because of your faithful love . . . (Psalm 6:2–5)

2. Start with Simple Prayer

God wants to help, but as our Master Physician, he needs to hear where you hurt.

Healing is a cooperative effort; you can't just expect the doctor to do all the work. Remember: pain is instructive. It's important that the patient reveal his or her pain so that the doctor can get to the true source of the problem. Only then will full healing be possible. Go to Him; don't be afraid to get up on the exam table and start talking!

3. Find a Same-Sex Friend

It's a myth that an opposite-sex friend will help. Listen to the men and women on the Survival Guide series share their painful heartbreak at rushing too soon into opposite-sex "friendships."

The highest form of friendship is a virtuous friendship in which two people are committed to helping each other live not the happiest of lives, but the holiest of lives.

Find a same-sex friend who is committed to living a holy life, and confide your sorrows to him or her.

_____

_____

_____

_____

_____

_____

_____

_____

Anger Is a Normal Response

Have you ever tried to take your car keys away from a toddler? The minute a child thinks you are depriving him or her of happiness or security, you're apt to hear screams of anger: *"No fair! Mo-o-om, he took my toy!"*

In divorce you can lose hope, security, love, peace, identity, dreams and plans for the future, homes, cars, cash, even your kids. The list can seem endless. And that will make you angry.

Remember that even Jesus got angry—but He allowed that emotion to move Him to right wrongs . . . not to move Him to bitterness, self-pity, or revenge.

The feeling of anger may not be a sin, but what we do with it can be.

Personal Reflections:

_____

_____

_____

_____

Loss Can Trigger Anger

In the Survival Guide series, we talk about "inordinate attachments"—hanging on too tightly to people, places, things, or even intangibles like dreams, hopes and expectations. Even though the things we want are good, nothing is as good as God.

If you panic or grab at or fight for something to the point that you make yourself sick with emotion—such as with anger—then you probably have made a "false idol" out of that desire; you have become inordinately attached to it. Ask God to help you let go.

When there's an emotional attachment, there will be an equal emotional response to the loss of that attachment.

It will either be anger . . . or sadness, which is often anger without energy.

Personal Reflections:

_____

_____

_____

_____

_____

_____

_____

_____

_____

_____

_____

_____

_____

_____

_____

_____

_____

_____

_____

_____

_____

_____

_____

_____

Anger Can Move You to Justice

Some things that make you angry will require that you take positive action to right a wrong.

- Is there a fear that is holding you back from doing what is right?
- Have you become passive, or lazy?

Sometimes the situation is beyond your control, but you'll need to learn to see when action is needed—or not.

- Why can't you let go or accept?
- Are you still expecting life to be fair?

Knowing when to act, and when not to, takes both prayer and practice.

Personal Reflections:

_____

_____

_____

_____

Anger Can Turn to Bitterness

Scripture says, "Be angry, but do not sin." (Ephesians 4:26)

If you've done all you can, then it's time to let go of the feelings of anger and let yourself grieve the loss. Otherwise, anger will turn to the sin of bitterness, whereby you focus on your pain and forget that God can be trusted even when the other person cannot. Bitterness is a deadly poison that will hurt you far more than it could ever hurt the other person.

Personal Reflections:

_____

_____

_____

_____

_____

_____

_____

_____

_____

Anger Must Be Released

People who carry loads of anger around don't always look angry from the outside. But too much food, sleep, work, or other self-medication can signal a quiet anger that is seething just below the surface.

Extroverted people usually show their anger.
Introverted people usually keep it inside.

The best thing you can do is ask God to show you where anger in your life needs Confession and grace. Then His sweet mercy will replace the bitterness in your life. Is Jesus asking you to come see Him in the healing, releasing, powerful gift of Confession (Sacrament of Reconciliation)?

Personal Reflections:

_____

_____

_____

_____

_____

1. Make a List of Losses

Keep a tablet with you for a week: in the car, at work, at home. Or use the note pages in this Survival Guide.

As you become aware of them, write down all the losses that come with divorce, in every area of your life.

Losses that can make you angry: love, intimacy, companionship, future, security, hope, friends, family, position in the community, homes, cars, bank accounts, credit ratings, Church ministry, holiday traditions . . .

You might be surprised how big the list is!

2. Ask God for the Grace to Grieve

We don't grieve well in our culture; we either hide it or hurl it at others—or swing back and forth between the two extremes.

Our culture has lied to us about what it means to be human, and as a result we feel uncomfortable with the natural grieving process God gave us:

"Big boys (and girls) don't cry." "Stop crying—here's a sucker." "Suck it up and get over it—move on."

But other cultures know the great physical, emotional, and spiritual release that comes from appropriate mourning periods, rites, and rituals. Tears are for cleansing.

Ask God for the grace for healthy grieving that can relieve your hurt, pain, stress . . . and anger.

3. Offer God Your Losses

It's called "redemptive suffering": from Christ's pain came the fruits of our salvation, and so, too, can your loss and pain produce spiritual fruit.

Here's how it works: Imagine Jesus' blood flowing like a life-giving fountain from the cross. Throughout time (and outside time and space) that blood is still giving eternal life, immeasurable grace, healing, and blessings, to men and women in the past, present, and future.

Now, you can let your emotional blood from divorce spill to the ground and cry over it—or you can unite your pain with His so that it has power for redemption for you and others. Don't just "lay it at the foot of the cross": climb up there and put your arms around Him. Press your pain into His, uniting the injustices done to you, through divorce, with those done to Him.

_____

_____

_____

_____

_____

Isolation Is Sometimes Necessary

Time off to heal is absolutely necessary. Even Jesus got away from everyone, went up to the hillside of Jerusalem, and cried over His lost sheep. He knew that time alone helped Him draw closer to His Father so that He could be recharged. But check to see why you are isolating (or refusing to isolate):

- You might be withdrawing from reality.
- You might be afraid to be alone, always with someone, anyone!

Regardless, don't feel guilty about needing to pull back from others for a while to take the time to heal. And remember: full healing comes with spending that "alone" time in the presence of God.

Personal Reflections:

_____

_____

_____

_____

_____

Depression Is Different for Everyone

Depression can take many forms and can come at different times. Depression gives us "down" time to heal; the problem comes when we get stuck in it for long periods of time.

Depressed people don't always look depressed; it depends on the degree of their attachments in the marriage and on their natural temperament. You never know when that happy-go-lucky or class-clown type may be on the verge of tears. And some personalities naturally like a little melancholy!

Personal Reflections:

_____

_____

_____

_____

_____

_____

_____

Feelings Can Paralyze You

Hiding at home and feeling hopeless can sometimes be easier than facing your fears. It's scary to think of being alone, of losing everything, of never being loved again. Those fears can paralyze people.

Fears may not always be based on reality. Jesus said over and over and over, "Do not be afraid . . . I am with you."

Remember when the disciples were being pounded in an angry wind storm at sea? Jesus mysteriously appeared and told them to take courage, assuring them that He was with them. And the storm died down. (Mark 6:51)

The storm after your divorce may still be raging around you, but the one in your heart will die down when you begin to trust God.

Personal Reflections:

_____

_____

_____

_____

Mourning and Meds Can Help

Humans are visible flesh and blood, and invisible mind and spirit. What affects one usually affects the other: most people need help for depression in all areas. Some forms of depression can start when your chemical makeup gets out of whack. You may need the help God provides through doctors and medication to stabilize you. But other forms of depression start in the mind and heart. Some of it stems from lack of knowledge and wrong thinking. Healing for that can come from a good Spiritual Director or therapist, or both.

No matter where depression begins, both your body and soul can suffer. Don't be afraid of medication, and don't avoid a good Catholic therapist's couch!

Personal Reflections:

_____

_____

_____

_____

_____

_____

Despair Is Not an Option

Depression can be healthy; despair is not. Despair believes the lies that you are alone, that no one cares, that there is no help, that there is no end in sight.

Clearly this flies in the face of our Catholic faith: you are not alone! God cares more than you know, and He wants to help, usually through other people. There is hope. Even though you don't feel it, you must believe it.

Personal Reflections:

_____

_____

_____

_____

_____

_____

_____

_____

_____

1. Don't Be Afraid to Grieve

Some people absolutely refuse to let down. They see grief, mourning, and crying as weakness. They are so afraid of what others think, or are trying so hard to maintain their image— maybe even to themselves—that they stay emotionally "constipated." But all that does is bring more pain!

- If you need to cry—and can't—go rent a tear-jerking movie.
- Maybe you need to get really angry before tears come.
- Maybe you need to stop trying to be so perfect.
- Maybe you just need to slow down a little, and let it come.

Ask God to reveal any pride that keeps you from healthy and appropriate grieving.

2. Get Professional Help

Depression is different for everyone, and God will use His people to bring His healing touch in just the way you need it.

He might have a good therapist, spiritual director, or medical doctor waiting to help you. What are you waiting for?

www.CatholicTherapists.com

www.DrRay.com

www.CatholicSpiritualDirection.org

3. Unite Your Pain with His

We can't repeat too often the long-taught, Catholic concept of "redemptive suffering":

St. Paul says that we need to join with Christ on the cross to help complete His work (Colossians 1:24). Jesus has always wanted us to participate with Him in redeeming hearts and souls. After all, love desires union!

That means taking all the pain and allowing Christ to make something beautiful from it that will bless the whole Church. The gifts of our intellect, emotions, will, and imagination can help.

Imagine Jesus with outstretched arms, still with gaping, bleeding hands. Take His hands. Let your blood mingle with His, and He will bring deep healing from it. He conquered death; with His help you can conquer depression.

_____

_____

_____

_____

_____

PART 2

Finding Perfect Power

Session 5: Learning to Forgive
Session 6: Dealing with Your Family
Session 7: Handling Money Wisely
Session 8: Finding Perfect Power

You may still be involved in visitation arguments, court battles, or ongoing support or other crucial money issues. There are problems with your ex or with other family members, or your kids are acting out and crying for help in many different ways. It seems that peace will never come.

But true Peace is not about Christ coming into your life to change your ex, build up your bank account, or bring you the new love of your life. True Peace is about you abiding in Him, knowing His love and understanding where you are headed despite the world around you. It's not about Him calming the storm as much as it is about Him standing by you in the midst of it.

Only when you're able to stand with Christ in the storm will you be able to tackle head-on the issues of your ex, the courts, the kids, and new relationships. The interior power you'll need comes only by having His peace within your heart.

Forgiveness Is a Command

Forgiveness is a command, not a suggestion. Jesus said quite clearly that unless we forgive others, we make it impossible for Him to forgive us. Look up: Matthew 6:15, Mark 11:26.

When we hesitate—even refuse—to forgive, we assume the position of God for ourselves . . . and, sorry, folks: that job is already taken.

Personal Reflections:

_____

_____

_____

_____

_____

_____

_____

_____

Forgiveness Is Not a Feeling

Remember what we learned in the sessions on peace: emotions come and go; it is our intellect (right thinking) that must be the basis for our life and actions.

The Catechism of the Catholic Church (CCC) teaches that emotions in themselves are neither good nor evil, but must be controlled by the will. And we are promised that the Holy Spirit will give us the power to do what is right, even when we don't feel like it. (CCC 1767–1769)

Many times you will not feel like forgiving, but by your baptism, you have the power of God to assent in your will by saying: "Lord, I do forgive that person."

Personal Reflections:

_____

_____

_____

_____

_____

Forgiveness Doesn't Cancel Justice

Sometimes we refuse to forgive, because we think that if we do, the other person gets off scot-free, and that's just not fair! So . . . not believing (or trusting) that God will take care of it in His perfect way and time, we withhold forgiveness as punishment, or so that we can feel in control. But that's really a lack of faith and trust in God's justice.

Don't worry: your desire for justice has its root in your heart's desire for God Himself, Who is perfect Justice . . . and perfect Mercy.

The trouble starts when you want justice in your way, and according to your timetable. Be generous with your forgiveness, and God will be generous with you.

Personal Reflections:

_____

_____

_____

_____

_____

Forgiveness Doesn't Mean Trusting the Other Person

If you know someone may keep hurting you, you have an obligation to learn how to set and keep healthy boundaries, without an ungodly attitude. Stay cautious, and be smart. Jesus said you might be like a sheep among the wolves, but instead of being a victim you should be as wise and cunning as a serpent, yet gentle (not weak—but loving) as doves (Matthew 10:16). You might never be able to trust the other person, but that does not mean you should not forgive.

Yes, people need to earn your trust . . . but no one needs to earn forgiveness.

Personal Reflections:

_____

_____

_____

_____

_____

_____

_____

Forgiveness Is a Gift You Give to Yourself

When you don't forgive, you keep yourself stuck at your greatest point of pain.

In our series, author and theologian Christopher West shares that "pain is instructive": it's there to show us that something needs changing, fixing, healing, or redeeming. But some people actually like the emotional "payoff" of suffering, hurt, or anger, and they choose to stay there, with their finger pointed at the other person. Forgiveness is freedom from that pain.

Personal Reflections:

_____

_____

_____

_____

_____

_____

_____

_____

1. Make a List of Those Whom You Should Forgive

Use good judgment on this; it can be prideful and arrogant to call someone up and say, "I forgive you!"

- Make a list of those who have hurt you, and take it to God.
- Don't wait for the feeling.
- Ask for the grace to let go.
- Keep adding to the list as new names come up.
- Wait to give the gift of forgiveness to others until they seek it.

Forgiveness begins in your head and heart and is first of all between you and God; if someone asks for forgiveness, you will already have it there, ready to be given.

_____

_____

_____

_____

_____

2. Seek Forgiveness from Others

Even when you have been extremely wronged, if you can search your heart from the times you failed others and ask for forgiveness, you will be on your way to sainthood! Make a list of those you have failed, and ask for their forgiveness. Rather than detail all your sins, you can ask forgiveness "for all the ways and all the times I failed to love you, respect you, and honor you." If you're embarrassed or afraid, place a phone call with a good friend sitting beside you. Although it's best to make a face-to-face request—if you can—or a phone call, in some cases, a letter will do. Don't get into a long talk or argument about the past; simply ask, "Will you forgive me?" and avoid any arguments that may ensue.

Some may not be ready for such a conversation; give them time, and let it go.

_____

_____

_____

_____

_____

3. Receive Forgiveness from God

Once you recognize from your lists that you have been
withholding love, mercy, or forgiveness, make your own list of
sins (Examination of Conscience), go to Confession, and ask
once again for God's pardon. Jesus breathed the Holy Spirit
onto the Apostles and commanded them to forgive sins (John
20: 22–23). How could they—the first ministerial priests—
forgive sins without first hearing them?

We must overcome our fear, shame, and pride to meet Jesus
personally and powerfully in the Sacrament.

Frequent Confession will build the virtue of true humility
in you; it will strengthen you and empower you to love rightly.
Do it!

_____

_____

_____

_____

_____

Be Realistic about Your Ex

Your ex is no longer your spouse, and your expectations of him or her need to change; otherwise you will still be emotionally married . . . and that is a miserable place to be.

Ideally, some time in the future you can be cordial and helpful to one another in the parenting of your children. The key is to remember that this will most likely occur sometime in the future.

On at least one side, emotional wounds need to be healed first, and that may require distance, limited contact, and what appears to be a cool, businesslike relationship. Permit that. Receive that. And know that nothing stays the same forever.

Invite God in and allow Him to work in your heart in this area.

Personal Reflections:

_____

_____

_____

_____

Be Your Kids' Parent First

This may sound harsh, but although friendship is certainly a part of your relationship with your kids, it is not your primary responsibility.

• God wants you to lead your kids to heaven, not to Disneyland.
• Your goal is not to make your kids happy, but holy.
• Overindulgent and permissive parenting is a real form of child abuse.

What kids need most is good role modeling from at least one parent who is centered in Christ and trying to live a structured and disciplined life of virtue and holiness.

Personal Reflections:

_____

_____

_____

_____

_____

_____

Heal Your Own Emotions First

It's one thing to be honest with children, but another to make them our emotional confidantes. Some parents make their children their "surrogate spouses," not in a sexual way but in an emotional one. Such parents share the details of the divorce, discuss the money problems with the kids, and begin to center their lives around the children. Big mistake.

If this happens, the kids have, in a certain sense, been reduced to "numbing agents" to ease the parent's pain and loneliness. The best thing you can do for your children is get an adult support system for yourself.

Read some good parenting books, like those written by Dr. Ray Guarendi. Then, strengthened and healing, you can be the rock your children need.

Personal Reflections:

_____

_____

_____

_____

_____

Teach Your Kids through Divorce

Your kids experience divorce differently than you do, for many reasons—one being that they are unique and unrepeatable human persons. But, like you, your children will probably find their emotions to be up and down, and you may experience lots of acting out, withdrawal, or other such changes.

Make sure there are regular meals, regular bedtimes, and lots of time to just sit down and talk. And change any overly structured schedules—that will only delay family healing. Kids don't need to play every sport or join every club, and even none at all for a while might be good for everyone.

And teach your children what you learn through this divorce, so that maybe one day God can use them to bring His love and healing to others.

Personal Reflections:

_____

_____

_____

_____

Let Your Kids Love Others

Never, ever, ever bad-mouth the other parent to your children!

The best gift you can give your children is to love their other parent—even after a divorce.

Yes, the kids might get hurt, let down, betrayed . . . but instead of overprotecting them, walk them through the bumpy parts of their relationship with their mom or dad. Kids are smart—they will figure out the truth a lot faster than you think.

And if they have a new family, including a step-parent or step-siblings, be mature enough to encourage their love for those people, too.

Personal Reflections:

_____

_____

_____

_____

1. Redefine Your Ex

In God's perfect order, we are not meant to be ex-spouses, but in our fallen world we need to come up with a way of seeing the other person that is loving and appropriate—but not as a spouse.

This will help avoid confusion for you, your ex-spouse, and your children.

This is important: truly loving an ex-spouse the way God loves him or her does not mean relating to them in the old, familiar, affectionate ways. Kids need to see you respect and care about one another, but they will be terribly confused and anxious (whether you realize it or not) when you still play at being married. Get some counseling on this if necessary.

_____

_____

_____

_____

_____

_____

2. Change Your Expectations

Make a list of all the things you expect from your ex and take it to your Spiritual Director or therapist, or to God in prayer. Or all of the above.

• Do you expect him or her to be different than when you were married?

• Do you still expect a birthday card?

• Do you expect unrealistic behavior from him or her?

• Do you think you can still call and request special favors?

• Are you waiting for an apology?

Decide which of your expectations are realistic, and which are not . . . and make some changes in the way you think.

_____

_____

_____

_____

_____

_____

3. Depend on Christ, Not Your Kids

Your children don't really belong to you—they belong to God. He has entrusted you with their care for a short time in their lives so that they can know His love through your love, pointing them toward heaven. But they are meant to leave the nest some day. Despite the divorce, God wants you to continue getting them ready for the world. But you're tired, angry, sad, alone, and longing for love and stability. Your kids can seem to provide that for a while. But He is the one your heart really desires.

Instead of grabbing out frantically for the love of your children, reach out for the hem of His garment. Then you'll have something of eternal value to pass on to your children.

_____

_____

_____

_____

_____

_____

_____

Love of Money Is Evil

The bible does not say that money is the root of all evil, but it does say that the love of money is the root of all evil.

For the love of money is the root of all evils, and some people in their desire for it have strayed from the faith and have pierced themselves with many pains (1 Timothy 6:10).

We've talked about this already: "evil" can be seen as the disordered view that something is so important to us it becomes a false god; it keeps us from trusting in God's provision. Well, money certainly has a way of doing that! Do you have an "inordinate attachment" to money and possessions? What fears about money—or provisions—are still keeping you enslaved?

Personal Reflections:

_____

_____

_____

_____

_____

Your Money Belongs to God

God has given you every good gift, including money. It is yours to take care of the basics and to be generous with others. Period. Nothing else. It really belongs to Him.

There are lots of parables in Scripture about the landowner or the master giving money or resources to his servants and seeing what they would do with it. He is still our Master, and our money is still His. What will you do with it?

Personal Reflections:

_____

_____

_____

_____

_____

_____

_____

_____

_____

Take Care of First Things First

The basics of moderate food, clothing, shelter, and health care come first. Everything else ... everything ... is not a need, but a want. Ask God to help you see past our culture's seductive lies of more, more, more and get back to basics.

Why don't you begin to say "no" to more things and teach your children the virtues of self-control, self-discipline, and self-denial. You'll be preparing them to be good future spouses! And if you owe money to the other parent for child support, pay it.

Personal Reflections:

_____

_____

_____

_____

_____

_____

_____

_____

Less Is Really More

How many Christmas presents does a child really need? I remember one year my stepson opened about a hundred presents and then whined, "Is that all?"

- Have you overindulged your children?
- Have you accumulated closets and garages full of "stuff"?
- Where can you begin to give it all away?

There is a tremendous freedom in being detached: not rejecting material goods, but holding them loosely.

Personal Reflections:

_____

_____

_____

_____

_____

_____

_____

You Can't Take It with You

Do you ever wonder why many of the saints lived lives of utter simplicity?

As they matured, they began to realize that material goods are important, but not always necessary.

They began to willingly shed their attachments to things and reach out more for eternal riches right here on earth.

We need to start doing the same and then teaching it to our children.

Why don't you plan a big garage sale soon? Have the kids give away half their toys—or more!

Personal Reflections:

_____

_____

_____

_____

_____

1. Learn to Live on a Budget

If you're not living within your means, you're probably a slave to the fleeting happiness of things.

Get help with a budget and free yourself of loads of stress. Go to www.Catholic.org for loads of practical, easy help managing your money and getting out of debt.

If you're depending on the other parent for his or her check, I challenge you to learn to live without it: if it comes, put it into savings. If it doesn't, you're not panicked or locked in a dance of constant anger.

2. Learn to Say No

Living "within your means" means being able to say no to yourself and to your kids.

Think about it: What thinking keeps you afraid to say no? That you'll be a bad parent? That God can't be trusted to provide?

Self-denial is a Christian virtue and brings rewards beyond anything money can buy, like teaching your kids that God and love and goodness are more important than any thing.

3. Be Generous with Your Money

In the parable of the widow's mite, we see that even the poorest of the poor can gain by generosity of heart.

The whole meaning of life is love . . . and Jesus shows us that love is being a sincere gift of self to others. That means giving it freely and generously, as He does with His love, His mercy . . . and His very life . . . for us.

Even when it seems you have nothing left over to give, trust God and give anyway.

You just might be surprised to see what happens in your life!

_____

_____

_____

_____

_____

_____

_____

_____

Avoid Court If You Can

"Be willing to lose ... in order to win."

That's what Jesus did: paradoxically, He was willing to lose in order to win. He subjected Himself to suffering, humiliation, even death, because of something greater that He knew would come from it. Scripture says that if you're on your way to court, you should settle before you get there (Matthew 5:25). Make a list of all your assets, and then be generous and yielding with your ex-spouse. Even when it's not fair.

Sometimes you'll need a lawyer for complex issues, but even then, if your attorney (or others) tries to urge you into a drawn-out battle, let it go. Give in. Trust God to restore what you have lost.

Personal Reflections:

_____

_____

_____

_____

_____

SESSION 8 – SURVIVAL POINT 2
Know When to Fight—or Not

Some people avoid court for the wrong reason: they are afraid. They don't want to face reality, don't want to spend the money, don't think they can do it all on their own.

But sometimes you need to get a good attorney, on a limited basis. Every situation is different. Pray for the virtue of prudence: knowing when and when not to go to court.

Personal Reflections:

_____

_____

_____

_____

_____

_____

_____

_____

_____

Ask Only for What You Need

We have every right to ask and fight for justice, but never to the point that it keeps us emotionally attached, angry, and bitter.

Be reasonable in your request, but remember that perfect justice will not always happen here on Earth.

Don't be greedy.

Personal Reflections:

_____

_____

_____

_____

_____

_____

_____

_____

Be Generous with Time and Money

Give the other parent lots of time, on a reasonable basis, with the kids if they want it.

Despite his or her imperfections, your ex-spouse is your child's other parent. Don't be chintzy with visitation time. Let the kids go even when it's not in the visitation agreement.

Be willing to "lose" in order that you and your kids may "win" when they see you modeling a generous heart with their other parent.

Personal Reflections:

_____

_____

_____

_____

_____

_____

_____

1. Release Your Needs in Prayer

Prayer should not be our last resort, but our first.

Everyone needs to practice trust in God.

Try saying this throughout the day—even for the rest of your life:

"Sacred Heart of Jesus, I place my trust in Thee."

2. End Unnecessary Battles

Trusting God—or not—is the root of many problems in divorce, and in life in general.

Your trust may have been damaged as a child, and you may still operate on the basis of having to fend for yourself. Ask God for the grace to heal old thought patterns and to heal any deep emotional wounds that keep you from trusting in His Providence and His Justice.

When the battles are lingering, make a clear decision to initiate an end—go ahead and settle. And do it today. You'll never regret it.

3. Seek to Grow in Love

Saint John wrote, "Perfect love casts out fear" (1 John 4:18).

Your worries, fears, anger, doubt, resentments, and fighting will cease when you have love.

But love is not romance, friendship, or even getting along.

True love is a continual emptying of self for the good of another—maybe even someone you don't like or can't trust.

And that is a way of life that will give you unending freedom, constant joy, and perfect power.

_____

_____

_____

_____

_____

_____

_____

PART 3

Finding Perfect Passion

Session 9: Seeing God in Romance
Session 10: Relearning How to Date
Session 11: Loving All Church Teachings
Session 12: Finding Perfect Passion

Did you know that romance reveals the very meaning of the existence of life?

It's true . . . we were all made for love, to be a gift in our person to others, so that we could begin to experience and understand a little of God's sweet love and desire for us. He—the eternal Bridegroom—is the One who first loved us, and He pursues us (the Bride) every day, inviting us into His perfect love.

You can learn more about this spousal analogy in Pope John Paul II's beautiful work The Theology of the Body, which will show you the real reason your heart desires love.

God Proposes Love

Have you seen anyone in love lately? They smile at everyone, they don't get upset at anything, and they will often do whatever you say, even volunteer to do more. Their love just can't be contained; it affects and even softens almost everyone around them. True Love wants to just pour itself out onto others.

And that's what God's love does: it desires to pour itself out onto the world and bring us all into it.

Even if your heart has been damaged by divorce, it still remembers, at however deep a level, that call to come into God's love.

Personal Reflections:

_____

_____

_____

_____

_____

_____

True Love Is Always Faithful

Have you ever been betrayed in a relationship?

In the spousal analogy, all of mankind is in a bridal position of openness to a loving Husband (God). He wants to fill us with the seed of His eternal life so that we can bear that Love and Life to the world.

But our love story has a bad guy: the enemy who came into the Garden and seduced us away.

Adam and Eve didn't totally reject God, but they did turn their focus and loyalties away from Him, rejecting True Love for a counterfeit.

They put other things in higher order than God: it was the first divorce in the visible world.

Personal Reflections:

_____

_____

_____

_____

Sex Should Tell the Truth

If I smile and shake your hand in an agreement, but inside I am reserving my true thoughts (such as I have no intention of living up to the terms of this deal), then I am lying to you with my body. The outward physical act of shaking your hand in agreement is therefore deceptive, misleading, and always, at some level, hurtful.

When the outward act of sex appears to be saying, "Nothing stands between us—I give you my all," but in fact you are not giving your all, it is a lie. And lies always hurt. Sex is only meant as a sincere gift of self that is free (no agendas), total (nothing held back), faithful (safeguarding the heart of the other), and fruitful (open to life). And that can only exist in marriage between one man and one woman.

Personal Reflections:

_____

_____

_____

_____

_____

The Truth Will Set You Free

Speaking of lies, we've all been swallowing the lies about how to live, how to love, and how to find our own personal satisfaction. But guess what, we are increasingly, confused, sexually repressed (or addicted), chemically addicted, depressed, stressed, fat, sick. . . and more frequently divorced than ever!

Aren't you ready for the Truth? It's Jesus.

Personal Reflections:

_____

_____

_____

_____

_____

_____

_____

_____

_____

_____

Christ Redeems His Bride

In fairy tales, which usually have the salvation story as their basis, the hero always comes to the rescue of his bride.

And for our happily-ever-after, Jesus has come to save us.

Maybe now, from understanding this spousal analogy, you can see where real love and romance come from, and why we all long for romance in which the one who loves us never leaves us, never forsakes us, and, if necessary, would die for us.

Personal Reflections:

_____

_____

_____

_____

_____

_____

_____

1. Present Your Body to God

St. Paul urged the Romans to offer their bodies as living sacrifices to God (Romans 12:1–2).

We need to do the same thing. In a way, this body He gave us is His: we need to offer it back to Him and ask Him to fill us with grace so that we can love rightly, not hurt continually.

Tonight when you pray, why don't you try making a gift of your body and sexuality? Trust me. Great and beautiful things will begin to happen in your life!

2. Seek Greater Wisdom

Our series gives you just a little introduction to a glorious plan for your life, body, sexuality, and marriage that is richer than you could ever imagine.

Don't you want to know more? Our Web site has links to everything you ever wanted to know about the theology of your body. www.FaithLifeline.com

3. Guard Your Heart and Mind

If married love and sex are something that point you to a heavenly reality and a deeper love for God, who do you think wants to keep you from that?

Any time someone begins to turn away from the satanic lies of our culture of death to move toward the Truth about who we are as sexual beings, the enemy will push the lies harder, stir up your fears, and try to keep you confused.

Pray. Don't take these lies sitting down, but on your knees!

"St. Michael the Archangel, through the power of God, defend us in battle!"

_____

_____

_____

_____

_____

_____

If You Can't Marry, Then You Can't Date

If you're not ready in every area of your life to marry (and that includes a Church annulment), then you have no business dating. But, you may ask, what about "casual dating"? Sorry—there's no such thing as casual dating. Sure, you can go out and not yet know if a person is right for you or not, but even that is not truly casual. Whether with the intent of marriage or not, being with someone, getting their hopes up, and creating an environment with the potential for nurturing sexual intimacy is never casual.

Dating is serious business that involves a real person with a real heart. And if your divorce isn't final, you're still married! Don't you even think about dating "casually"—it's really a selfish use of another to ease your own loneliness.

Personal Reflections:

_____

_____

_____

_____

_____

Be Willing to Be Alone

Unless you are at peace with your own company, you're probably not ready to marry or date.

You may still see others as a way to fill your voids, to meet your emptiness, and that's a lot different than normal lonely time.

Having to always be with someone, or getting anxious because you have no weekend plans, is a huge red flag. What is it you really fear?

Personal Reflections:

_____

_____

_____

_____

_____

_____

Look for Things That Matter

Here we are with our lists again . . . but they help!

Make a list of all the things you desire in a spouse, and all the things you can't stand. Now boil each list down to the top ten (say) nonnegotiables. And when you're assessing a person as a possible spouse, make sure those lists list virtues, not body parts or bank accounts.

And then realize that this is only a guide: no person can ever be reduced to a list, but the list can help you see where you may be looking for the wrong things.

Personal Reflections:

_____

_____

_____

_____

_____

_____

_____

Take It Slowly

In an addictive need to fill the empty heart after a divorce, one person in a relationship may try to rush the dating process.

The other may drag his or her feet, still stuck in fear . . . quite possibly without the aid of a list, like the one discussed above, designed to aid in a purposeful search. Or perhaps both of you are moving at warp speed—or both at a snail's pace. Either pace may indicate that you may not really be ready.

Personal Reflections:

_____

_____

_____

_____

_____

_____

_____

_____

Commit to Doing It Right

Catholicism is rich in outward signs that bring our minds and hearts into inner spiritual realties. The "smells and bells," sights, sounds, colors, garments, and sacred vessels invite all our senses into our worship.

By now we hope you've made a firm decision to do things God's way in all areas of your life. So why not create your own rite of offering yourself to God in a fuller way than you've ever done before. You can use music, candles, or holy water.

Go ahead. In a special ceremony in the quiet of your own room, make a conscious decision to change, to surrender your head and heart to the way God has for you—and then thank Him for the grace He will send.

Personal Reflections:

_____

_____

_____

_____

_____

1. Keep Your Eyes Open

Being naive or overly optimistic, dreamy, or romantic is like wearing blinders. And being too physical too soon will bind you as well as blind you. Ask God where you may need His spiritual Visine!

2. Consider Staying Single

I know some have already made a decision to remain single, perhaps wisely or perhaps simply out of fear of future hurt. Think about it; pray about it; talk about it with your therapist or Spiritual Director. But don't let shutting the door on a new marriage make the children the center of your life or your reason for living—that's idolatry. And it will hurt your kids in the long run.

_____

_____

_____

_____

3. Avoid Playing at Marriage

Playing at marriage is really easy to slip into. It can include pizza together, watching videos as a family, even going to church together—but it can also move to sleeping together, hiding, sneaking, lying: telling yourself the Church's rules on sex are outdated. Puh-leez . . . aren't you ready to do things differently this time?

_____

_____

_____

_____

_____

_____

_____

_____

_____

Stay Open to the Truth

I went to twelve years of Catholic school, yet only today do I begin to see how much I did not know, and how much more I had to learn:

- Why sex outside marriage ultimately hurts
- What a Sacrament really is
- What marriage really is
- Why the annulment process is necessary

Today I'm in love with our faith. I have a newfound freedom and I'm excited! Like when you get a new computer and keep discovering all the new cool things you can do.

Don't think that just because you're Catholic you know it all already.

Personal Reflections:

_____

_____

_____

_____

_____

See the Church as Mother

A lot of you watching are parents: you know a good parent wants only the best for his or her children.

The Church in every sense of the word is our loving Mother. She's not perfect, but She knows what will keep us safe—and, moreover, really, really happy. Trust Her!

Personal Reflections:

_____

_____

_____

_____

_____

_____

_____

_____

_____

_____

_____

Seek Only to Be Holy

Do you want to be happy? Then strive to be holy.

No matter what questions or objections you have when it comes to life and love, the Church has the answers.

For the last two millennia, intelligent and holy men and women have left us lots of good advice, helpful hints on a sure path to true peace, power, and passion.

And our Church has preserved it in Sacred Scripture, in Sacred Tradition, and in the Catechism—and of course we put in our two cents' worth, too, on our Website!
www. FaithLifeline.com

Personal Reflections:

SESSION 11 – SURVIVAL POINT 4
Never Forget to Pray

There is a real enemy who wants you and your family to be lost and confused, without true Love.

And he hates the Church. He hates the warm, motherly Marian embrace into which we are called through the Church. And he wants to take Her down, by sowing doubt, confusion, and error.

So get on your knees. Learn to pray the Rosary, the powerful prayer of the Gospel.

Call out to heaven, to God and all his saints, and to St. Michael the Archangel, who will help you reject the counterfeits and find the Fullness of Truth that exists nowhere else but in the Catholic Church.

Personal Reflections:

_____

_____

_____

_____

_____

Find Peace in Confession

If you are the Bride of Christ, and called to receive Him into yourself at every Eucharist, don't you think you should come to Him looking your very best?

The shimmering white bridal gown and glorious beauty of the Bride should point us to the condition our soul should be in when we approach the altar to receive Jesus in the Eucharist.

Confessing your sins and allowing His grace to cleanse you and make you beautiful is the first act of love a Bride gives her Groom.

There's no peace like leaving the confessional with a clean slate. Get back to Confession and prepare your heart to receive Him in the Eucharist.

Personal Reflections:

_____

_____

_____

_____

1. List Your Main Objections

Still have an issue with the Church? That's okay.

Write down all the hard sayings and Church teachings with which you still struggle. Remember that it's hard to accept something that no one has ever fully explained to you!

Stay open and start researching, even a little at a time. The Catechism is a great place to start; your Spiritual Director can help, too.

2. Find Someone to Help

If you still can't understand or accept some Church teachings, get a friend who will help you, or sign up for an online forum at a good Catholic Web site, like Catholic Answers (www.Catholic.com).

And be careful. There are many misinformed people who call themselves Catholic (laity and clergy alike) who may lead you astray. Ask God to lead you.

3. Harden Not Your Heart

Eve had some questions about that hard-and-fast rule about the apple, but instead of discussing it with God, she didn't trust Him.

She may have thought, You know what—maybe God doesn't want me to be happy. Maybe he is holding something fun, exciting, powerful, or enticing back from me—maybe that nice serpent is right. He makes sense, doesn't he? And I have a mind of my own . . . right?

If today in Church teachings, if today in this survival guide, or that today you would hear His voice . . . Harden not your hearts" (Hebrews 3:8).

_____

_____

_____

_____

_____

_____

Our Destiny Is Heaven

Divorced men and women often believe they have forever lost that which would have made them truly happy. Or they again look to remarriage as the answer to all their problems. Many people seek a love that is fiery, passionate, and wild. But marriage is not our destiny; heaven is.

Marriage is made to show us a way to get to heaven, to enjoy a little taste of Love, security, warmth, and passion that will be totally fulfilled beyond our wildest imagination for all eternity. Now that's wild!

Personal Reflections:

_____

_____

_____

_____

_____

_____

_____

Jesus Is True Love

Look—it's pretty easy, really: as C.S. Lewis said, either Jesus is right, and is exactly who He says He is, or He's an outrageous liar, or simply crazy.

Jesus said, "I am the Way . . . the Truth . . . and the Life" (John 14:6).

So do you believe that, or not? He is the Way to Love, the Truth about Love, and the Life that only Love can generate in us. God is love—do you believe that?

Then why do you think you can find true love in all the wrong places? Because you're like me, like David, like St. Peter, like St. Paul, like Mother Teresa: we are all hobbling our crippled way to Love.

But, thank God, it is He who first loved us, and He who will bring us home.

Personal Reflections:

_____

_____

_____

No One Can Match His Love

One of the reasons we suffer divorce and other relationship problems is that we try to get all that God can give from a mere human being.

Ask God to show you "false idols"—for example, how you may have tried to get all your needs met through your ex-spouse or your children—and then seek forgiveness from Him for doing so. And if you're considering a new relationship, make sure you ask for the daily reminder that only God is God!

Personal Reflections:

_____

_____

_____

_____

_____

_____

_____

The Saints Can Point the Way

The beautiful Catholic doctrine of the Communion of Saints tells us that we are all bound in our love for Christ, and dead or alive, we are all still able to love and pray for one another. In Him, we are One.

St. Teresa of Avila and St. John of the Cross are two of my favorites. They experienced God in a way that is clearly spousal and marital, wild and passionate: not in a horizontal way (earthly), but in a vertical elevation of the heart, a passionate reaching toward heaven for an eternal embrace, a wild abandon for Christ. Why don't you make a point sometime soon to read some of their works?

Personal Reflections:

_____

_____

_____

_____

_____

He Feeds the Hungry Heart

Did you know that every good thing you desire is a pale image of the perfected version that is Jesus Christ Himself?

- Your desire for security is for Him, the Cornerstone.
- Your desire for strength is for Him, the Lion of Judah.
- Your desire for peace is for Him, the Prince of Peace.

Your desires for being well fed, for happiness, and for justice are all deep desires for all the attributes of the Son of God, of God Himself.

So the next time you swell with desire for anything or anyone, remember that your temporary satisfaction will be sweet but small—and, like Chinese food, you'll still be hungry afterward!

Jesus is the Bread of Life. Feed on Him.

Personal Reflections:

_____

_____

_____

1. Keep the Big Picture in Mind

In all your movements through the healing of divorce and trying to find true love, remember that the here and now is not eternity—and never will be.

Keep the big picture in mind, and all the little things will fall into place.

2. Let Him Direct Your Path

A loving Husband God would never let his Bride fall to any harm. Although the spousal analogy in Scripture is the most frequently used picture of the love of God for us, many other pictures are provided of how God loves us. Jesus is also portrayed as the Good Shepherd, and we are his flock.

The culture wants to pull you away from His protection. Don't be a dumb sheep and wander off the edge of a cliff!

Trust in the Lord with all your heart,
on your own intelligence rely not;
In all your ways be mindful of him,
and he will make straight your paths.
　-Proverbs 3:5–6

3. Trust God with All Your Heart

It takes a lifetime to move the human heart away from the lies, the hurt, and the counterfeits.

But keep moving! Take a day at a time.

Let the Church teach you. Let the Sacraments nourish you. Let the angels and Saints love you. And pray this prayer often:

"Sacred Heart of Jesus, I place my Trust in Thee."

_____

_____

_____

_____

_____

_____

_____

_____

_____

We're Here for You!

All of us involved with the Catholic's DIVORCE SURVIVAL Guide hope you've come away with a renewed sense of hope, and with some good practical survival tips.

Please remember that our Web site, www.FaithLifeline.com, has many more resources that you'll find helpful. And won't you tell a divorced friend about this series?

I know God has a lot more for you in the future, and I hope He brings you the desires of your heart. Until then, know that I hold you in my heart, and I pray daily for all who watch this series.

May all the glory be to the Father, and the Son, and the Holy Spirit. As it was in the beginning is now and ever shall be, world without end. Amen.

God bless you!